My First Pet

Birds

by Cari Meister

Bullfrog Books

Ideas for Parents and Teachers

Bullfrog Books let children practice reading informational text at the earliest reading levels. Repetition, familiar words, and photo labels support early readers.

Before Reading

- Ask the child to think about pet birds. Ask: What do you know about pet birds?

- Look at the picture glossary together. Read and discuss the words.

Read the Book

- "Walk" through the book and look at the photos. Let the child ask questions. Point out the photo labels.

- Read the book to the child, or have him or her read independently.

After Reading

- Prompt the child to think more. Ask: What do you need to take care of a bird? Would you like to own a bird?

Bullfrog Books are published by Jump!
5357 Penn Avenue South
Minneapolis, MN 55419
www.jumplibrary.com

Library of Congress Cataloging-in-Publication Data

Meister, Cari, author.
  Birds / by Cari Meister.
    pages cm. — (My first pet)
  Audience: 005-008.
  Audience: K to grade 3.
  Summary: "This photo-illustrated book for early readers tells how to take care of a pet bird and tells about a few types of birds that make good pets" — Provided by publisher.
  Includes bibliographical references and index.
  ISBN 978-1-62031-120-2 (hardcover) —
  ISBN 978-1-62496-187-8 (ebook) —
  ISBN 978-1-62031-141-7 (paperback)
  1. Cage birds — Juvenile literature.
  [1. Birds as pets.] I. Title.
  SF461.35.M45 2015
  636.6'8—dc23

2013042367

Series Editor: Rebecca Glaser
Series Designer: Ellen Huber
Book Designer: Anna Peterson
Photo Researcher: Casie Cook

Photo Credits: All photos by Shutterstock except: Alamy/Juniors Bildarchiv GmbH, 12–13; Dreamstime.com/Petrina Calabalic, 14–15; iStock, 22; SuperStock/Blue Jean Images, 19

Printed in the United States of America at Corporate Graphics, in North Mankato, Minnesota.
3-2014
10 9 8 7 6 5 4 3 2 1

Table of Contents

A New Pet

Jen wants a pet.

She gets a bird!

She buys a cage.

It has metal bars.

It has three perches.

metal
bars

perch

7

What kinds of birds are pets?

May has a macaw.

It climbs a rope toy.

rope

9

Kit has a finch.

Time to eat!

Kit feeds Herbert seeds.

She gives him water.

bird
seeds

11

Noah cleans Al's cage.

He puts in a
new cuttlebone.

Al will peck his
beak on it.

cuttlebone

Paco is a parakeet.

Lu gives him a peanut.

Paco says "Thank you."

Ethan wants his parakeet
to talk too.

He works with her
every day.

Lex lets his parrot fly.
She lands on his hand.

19

Birds are fun pets!

What Does a Bird Need?

perch
A place for birds to sit on, like rods or branches.

cage
A place where birds are kept so they can't fly away.

food
Small birds eat bird seed.

water dish
Birds need fresh, clean water every day.

toys
Birds need toys so they don't get bored.

cuttlebone
The inside shell of a cuttlefish; birds get calcium from it.

Picture Glossary

finch
A small seed-eating bird.

parakeet
A type of small parrot that has a long, tapered tail.

macaw
A brightly colored tropical parrot with a long tail.

parrot
A tropical bird with brightly colored feathers and a heavy, curved beak.

Index

To Learn More

Learning more is as easy as 1, 2, 3.

1) Go to www.factsurfer.com

2) Enter "pet bird" into the search box.

3) Click the "Surf" button to see a list of websites.

With factsurfer.com, finding more information is just a click away.